The Courage to Soar Behind Bars

Collected Stories from Women in Prison

PATRICE WEBER

Word Out Books
Eugene, Oregon

Published by Word Out Books
an imprint of
Winding Hall Publishers
PO Box 2689
Eugene OR 97402

Copyright © 2019 Patrice Weber

Cover Design by 8th Wonder Creations

All rights reserved. No part of this book may be reproduced or transmitted in any form or by any means, electronic or mechanical, including photocopying, recording, or stored in any information or retrieval system, without the prior written permission of the publisher, except as authorized by law.

ISBN-13: 978-1-947035-06-5

Printed in the United States of America

DEDICATION

I would like to dedicate this book to all the women who can relate to the struggle of being incarcerated. Who know what it's like to be "lock-up and lock-down," wanting to be free and waiting on your change to come…

Let me encourage you (my colleagues and my sorority sisters) to become creative. We all have special gifts and talents inside of us just waiting to be birthed. Don't sit around wasting time, waiting on God to make something happen for you. But instead, my sisters, God is waiting on you to take that first step and he will do the rest. You can start right where you are, locked up or free, with some paper and a pen. Pray, write the Vision and Slay because you were born to Win…

I hope that this book will inspire you, like it has inspired us to share our stories, from behind bars. Words of wisdom, think outside the box…

— Patrice Weber, 2019

ACKNOWLEDGMENTS

First and foremost, I would like to give God all the glory, all the honor, and all the praise for making what seemed impossible possible. Some people thought, and even said, it couldn't be done because at the time I was locked up behind bars. But I believed that with God all things are possible, and I knew in my heart what God had given unto me was unique and something special, a Vision. So, I kept my faith the size of a mustard seed and I believed, if I watered that seed, it would grow into something bigger than life—and here I am, leaving my mark and Making A Difference (M.A.D.), behind bars.

My attitude of gratitude is towards all the teachers at the FCI Tallahassee, Florida federal prison in the Education Department. Special thanks to all of you for teaching, instructing and preparing us, with the knowledge and the education we need to succeed in life, to become productive and better members of society.

Ms. Mayo (Education Technician), Ms. LaRose (Literacy Teacher), Ms. C. Pineirovigo (Literacy Teacher), Mrs. P. Silva (Business Education), Ms. Cronin (Literacy Teacher), Mr. Bush (Building Trades), Mr. Gordillo (Culinary Arts), and Mr. Coleman (Literacy Teacher). Thanks to all of you for being a part of our journey in so many positive and influential ways.

To all the ladies who contributed a brief story of yourselves in this book, I'm grateful for all of you. I couldn't have done this without you. When others didn't believe in me and this book, y'all did! And we didn't allow the fear of our past to dictate to us by keeping us silent. But today we all know from experience that those life lessons are just Blessings in disguise...

> "Success isn't about how much money you make, it's about the difference you make in people's lives."
> — Michelle Obama

Special thanks to Brittany C. Wallace (Dear Mama), Tashira L. Garrett (Untitled), Shakayla Taylor (Living Through the Pain), Jessica Dorne (From Me, To You), Kisha E. Singletary (Rich in Spirit), Mallori Moss (1 way 2 live 2 no way out), Tetria N. Hill (Order out of Chaos), Jerrisha Rawlins (Dreams Worth More Than Money), Mona' Li (Letter to My Clyde), Sandra Simon (Club Paradise), Jaqualah Banks (Saabir the Great), Victorian L. Redwine (Who Am I), Denise Keaton (From Heels to Medical School), Jessica Nicholas (Finding Myself), and last but not least, Patrice Weber (My Life).

Thanks to all of you, for having

The Courage To Soar Behind Bars

Federal Bureau of Prison (FBOP)
vs.
Females Building on Purpose (FBOP)

INTRODUCTION

The Courage to Soar Behind Bars is a collaboration of stories from incarcerated women demonstrating a mental and moral strength to face their pasts, presents, and futures without fear. Using the gift of lived experience, turbulence, and confusion, and crafting it into the art of literacy in such a highly-controlled environment, these women have come together without any noticeable movement, penetrating barriers with their stories and lyrical combinations, rising higher than most can imagine, speaking on uncomfortable topics with equal importance, such as abuse, love, manipulation, and desperation, while unraveling the nurture vs. nature wiring behind our evolution.

This is a book in which just about every woman can find, if not a lesson, then solace in knowing they are not alone. Through these stories we are able to take a look at how much more we all have in common than not. You will be privileged to get a glimpse into these precious lives that haven't always been cherished or appreciated as such. With an open mind, or more importantly, an open heart we may realize that love and compassion can go a long way in this world. Love and compassion have the power to transform lives and so, sadly, if more had been given to some of these bent-but-not-yet-broken women, circumstances may have been drastically different for some of the ladies you will read about.

Nevertheless, we are all born into families and situations that we are unable to choose or change and for most it takes years of heartache, pain, and self-destruction before we are able to realize just how much of everything we thought we needed was already right there within us the whole time. We feel as if we are destined to repeat the destructive behavior of our parents or the unhealthy relationship patterns we are forced to be around, and more often than not, we do.

Fortunately, once we are able to become aware of the fact that there is something more powerful than our situations or ourselves, then and only then will we be able to gain the wisdom to know that we can have all of our hearts' desires as long as we choose so. Even though we may not always understand one another we can all learn from one another, and deep down we all need one another. We are all a part of this universe. We are all one energy that never dies, just passes on to another form. We are all interconnected in some way and whether we care to accept this fact or not, at the end of the day it is still just that, a fact.

"I learned long ago that in order to heal my wounds, I must have the courage to face up to them."
— Paulo Coelho, *Aleph*

CONTENTS

Dedication	iii
Acknowledgements	iv
Introduction	vii
Dear Mama — Brittany Cherice Wallace	1
Untitled — Tashira L. Garrett	7
Living Through the Pain — Shakayla Taylor	11
From Me, To You — Jessica Dorne	15
Rich in Spirit — Kisha E. Singletary	19
1 way 2 live 2 no way out — Mallori "Bunny" Moss	23
Order Out of Chaos — Tetria N. Hill	35
Dreams Worth More Than Money — Jerrisha "Risha" Rawlins ("CoCo")	39

Letter to My Clyde — Mona' Li   45

Club Paradise — Sandra Simon   51

Saabir the Great — Jaquala Banks   57

Who Am I — Victorian L. Redwine   62

From Heels to Medical School — Denise Keaton   65

Finding Myself — Jessica Nicholas   73

My Life — Patrice Weber   79

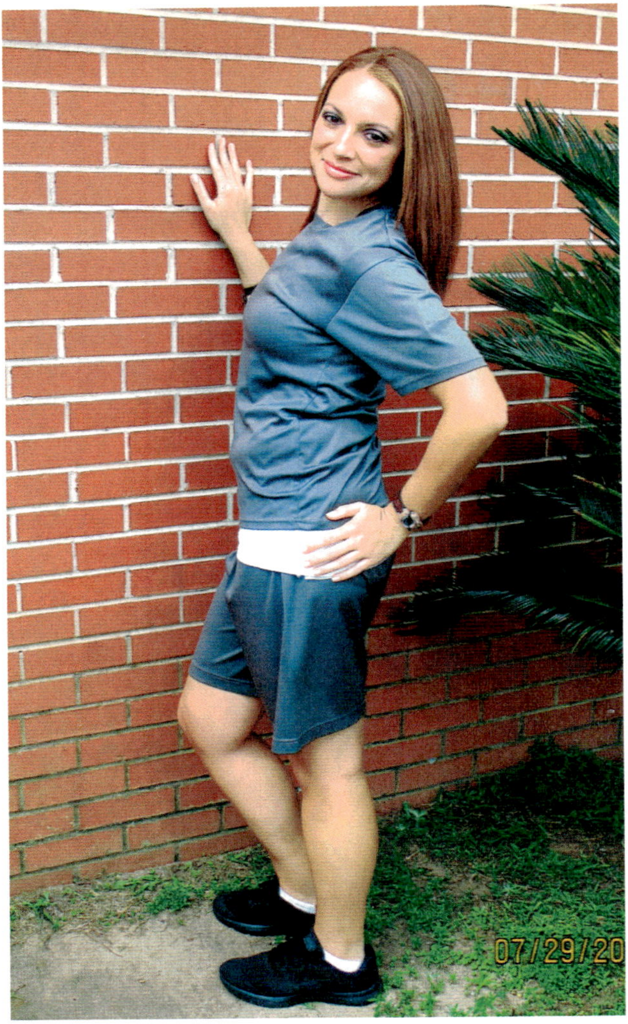
07/29/20

DEAR MAMA

Brittany Cherice Wallace

It's funny how growing up we have so many hopes and dreams for ourselves. In elementary I remember being asked what I wanted to be when I grew up. The answers varied throughout the class, from teachers to doctors to football and basketball stars. There seemed to be no limit to the success we could have as kids. Out of all of the many different places we saw ourselves, in prison was never one of them.

Now, sitting in federal prison, Tupac's "Dear Mama" hits close to home. The lyrics where he asks who thought in elementary they'd see the penitentiary one day are what I'm sure every man and woman has thought about at least once during their incarceration. No one says, as a child, I want to be a criminal, but yet in America, "the land of the free" as they call it, we lock up more people than any other country in the world. Now, sitting here at the age of twenty-five, nearing the end of my ten-year federal prison sentence that I started at the age of eighteen, I ask myself, why that is? Why are we building more prisons than we are schools or churches? Why is it that we can sentence someone who is eighteen or nineteen years old to ten, twenty, or more years in prison as a first time offender when they never raped or killed anyone, but yet rapists and murderers can get less time? Why do we give drug dealers more time than murderers?

You know why? Because it's a business. It's a money-making business that cares more about filling pockets which can never be satisfied, and proving a point that they are in control, than they care about the thousands upon thousands of children growing up not only without fathers as it seemed to be as I was growing up, but now without mothers as well. To me you can never justify giving someone a life sentence for selling drugs in order to feed their families, especially when you're not willing or able to provide them with a job.

True enough, there are some people in prison who are just greedy people that are all about satisfying themselves, but they're no different than most politicians or free people that could have also sat in our shoes. It was just by the grace of God or the fact that they knew "the right people" or came from "the right family" that they aren't.

Growing up, my great-grandmother used to always tell us, "Anyone is capable of anything." I never realized just how true that was until I landed here. Although being in prison was the last place I ever saw myself or would ever want to be, I take in all that I can, from the good to the bad. I take it all as a learning experience that I've grown from in so many ways. I've heard on multiple occasions that you are stuck at whatever age you were at the time of your incarceration and in some ways I see the logic behind this belief, being that the world as we once knew it will no longer be the same once we're released, but I also see this being so far from the truth. I'm nothing like the eighteen-year-old I once was at the beginning of my incarceration. That angry, bitter teenager who blamed everyone else for her problems no longer exists. So how is it that I'm stuck? All of the issues and insecurities I had at eighteen haven't completely disappeared, but thanks to my constant search for knowledge and meaning in life I'm far better equipped to deal with any negative feelings or thoughts, whereas at eighteen I was so lost I had no idea which way was up. My self-esteem and self-worth was so low I didn't care what happened to me which is what led me to prison in the first place. I had no one to tell me I deserved great things in life, but since going through this journey I've been taught by other beautiful women to tell myself.

So, no, you would never be able to convince me that I'm stuck when I see so much growth not only within myself, but also within many of the women I've been around for years. I've met women from all backgrounds. From a former stockbroker on Wall Street who is not only a black, Haitian-born woman, but also speaks English, French, and Spanish fluently, to a nun standing up for what she believed to be right, to doctors, paralegals, soldiers, victims, and addicts, to your average single mom just trying to get by. No matter the background or where we stand now we all have one thing in common. We still have that child within us with all of those same hopes and dreams. We may see more obstacles in our way than when things seemed much simpler in life, but with the right determination and with the right people surrounding us, there's still no limits to the things we can do. We have to stop blaming and start forgiving. Stop waiting on the government to open their eyes to an epidemic of mass incarceration they may always turn a blind eye to, but always remember that there is power in numbers. So instead of us forgetting where we've been due to guilt, shame, or being unable to forgive ourselves, we have to always remember in order to always know where we are going.

Thank you to everyone who believes in mercy and not only second chances, but third and fourths as well. Thank you to everyone fighting for the marginalized, may you continue doing so and may the light within you forever continue to shine! God bless!

To my daughter, Serenity, may your light always shine bright!

By: Brittany Cherice Wallace, June 8th, 2018
#43499-074

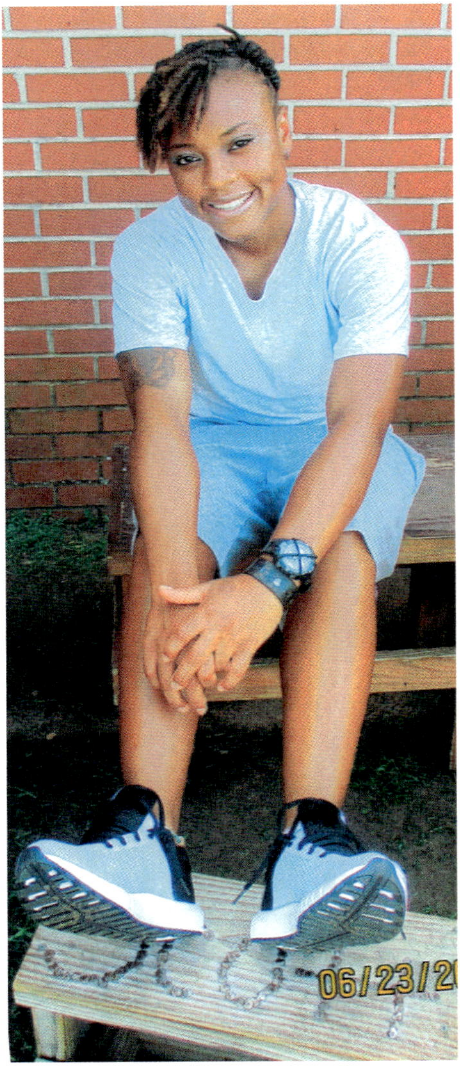
06/23/2

UNTITLED

Tashira L. Garrett

I never thought this life I'm living at the moment would come about. Being twenty-four years old caught by the Feds, now behind a prison fence, I think about the dreams and life I really wanted to live. I graduated high school on time and signed up for the Air Force. Having goals and doing something that can make a difference for me and my family was the plan, but the decisions life can bring can put you in a lot of life-or-death situations.

Being young and thinking that I was in love was a foolish thing. It also was a weak thing for me not realizing that loving someone and being there for them could come with a lot of hard repercussions. I tend to give my all, leaving my roots and the way I was raised behind me. I wasn't thinking about myself or my future plans. I wasn't taking it into consideration that I had family and friends that cared and loved me unconditionally. Why couldn't I feel and see that? Why did I have to be attracted to a lifestyle that was so out of my league to the point of destruction? Those are the questions I ask myself as I'm doing this time. I feel that the answers are not far behind. I have been realizing that things are not a coincidence and I've been learning about a powerful Creator called God who doesn't make any mistakes. He has shown me that my life at the moment is a part of the purpose he has before me. He's shown that there's a reason for things to come about. It's in order to truly see who I am and what it is for me to fulfill. I feel alive again. I was lost, but now I am found.

Decisions are a part of life. Good or bad, they all have an outcome. You may not always make the right decision, but it's what you do after that matters the most. Even though I'm in prison I'm not sitting on my ass pouting and depressed, waiting to be released. I'm learning and challenging my thoughts. I'm seeking out everything within myself that God created and bringing it out so that I can make a difference. From working my body out to see the physical aspects of how I can get into ship-shape and even shape others, to working a trade and learning skills to help me own a business. I'm even meeting people taking recovery classes, grasping on wisdom and giving wisdom to others in order to make a difference. I don't really know what it is, but I know one thing. I'm doing it. I'm doing whatever I can to better myself because life does not stop. It doesn't matter where you are or how many bad decisions you make in your life. It doesn't matter who you're with or where you've been. It's what you do after everything you have done. The man above has shown me that. I have taken all the biblical stories in as insight to live a better life within this satanic world.

It all starts with me letting go and letting God, forgiving, trusting, praising, worshipping, and most importantly, having faith. Those things can release a powerful force within you. Not only will you get your mind right, but you will make decisions that will take you to the highest peak of your ability. It's a beautiful thing that, now going on five years in prison, I'm ready to take life back on and see what I am meant to accomplish in this lifetime. I have an armor put on that is untouchable and I can finally say I have some answers to my questions. I have taken life as it is and I have learned that decisions I have made in my life cannot define me unless I let them. For those reasons I am grateful.

Take all that is going on in your life and find the good. Take out the bad and the ugly and make a difference. If you believe the Lord has your back he will always give you a way out. Don't ever give up and keep fighting, and remember that everything evil you do you will pay back someday.

To my family and friends, it's never too late to accept change. Love you and may the Lord be with you.

Tashira L. Garrett
#28992-064

03/17/2018 13:05

LIVING THROUGH THE PAIN

Shakayla Taylor

I graduated from West Port High School with a 4.5 G.P.A. I had already secured my Florida Opportunity Scholarship from the University of Florida and time was in my favor. I was "smart." I knew that, but did I really have the potential to become the best female African-American criminal defense attorney the world had ever seen? That I did not know, but they were truly going to find out.

College was a little more difficult than I thought. One semester I wanted to be a lawyer, the next semester a speech language pathologist didn't sound too bad. I was all over the place. Philosophy is the major I stuck with in the hopes of becoming a lawyer.

I joined Phi Alpha Delta, a pre-law fraternity, to help enhance my knowledge in my field. I learned a lot from my colleagues and with the help of them I made it far.

Rest in peace, Aira. My first dear roommate from Beauty Towers. You are forever in my heart. Your family forever in my prayers. I thought my tears would never end as I told my grandma about the passing of Aira. Little did I know her time was dwindling as well. When September 26, 2013, the worst day of my life, came I hit rock bottom.

Nothing mattered, because my grandma was gone. I skipped out of my classes, called out of work, and looked for a way out.

November, 2013 I met "him." My co-defendant. He took my mind out of a dark place and showed me that love and affection that I always wanted. In the beginning everything was so perfect, so I thought, until his girlfriend that he said he did not have came into the picture.

Three years of hurt, betrayal, pain, loneliness, and anger. Yes, so much anger and fury. I hit another rough patch. Prison saved my life. The time would have come down to whether it was his life or my life and the Lord saved us both.

I have learned that respect and loyalty can stand the test of time. The people who are not truly for you will fade away. Not saying that everyone's intentions are bad, but how many can you say are actually good? In prison I have learned the hard way who is for me and who is not. I did not allow my situation to control me. I have held a steady job for over a year now and participated in over 15 programs to better myself. Every day is a new opportunity to make me a better me. I wake up and put a smile on my face, faithfully. I love me, and the person that I am is truly happy.

No matter what, I encourage you to be the best that you can be. Believe in yourself and know that God is in control. I would like to thank my mother, my stepfather, my three little brothers, my father, and stepmother. No matter what happens in life I encourage you to be the best that you can be. Believe in yourself and know that God is in control.

Shakayla Taylor
#23750-017

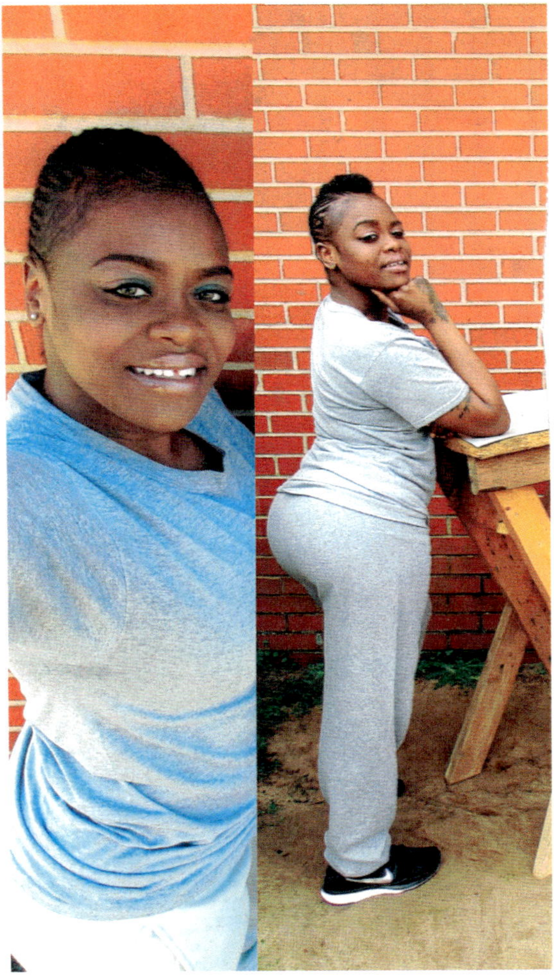

FROM ME, TO YOU

Jessica Dorne

Today I turned 25 years old. Unfortunately, this is my second birthday in prison. Let's face it, all time is hard time. But this part of my life has been the most dehumanizing. God knows that if it wasn't for this prison experience I would have been dead.

I had it very rough growing up. I'm the one they call "the Black Sheep" in my family. I'm a Haitian-American woman from West Palm Beach, FL. I live in a tough part of town, it's what most people call the "hood." Out there it's killed or be killed. To me it's only two ways to make it out the hood, and that's college or prison.

Growing up, I always had dreams of becoming a doctor, but instead I became a high school dropout. With my Security Guard and Home Health Aide licenses, I still managed to take care of myself. I personally struggle with sentimentality so that just wasn't enough money to take care of my family and me. My life was okay until I got the most disturbing news about my mother and how she had just gotten arrested in Haiti. So I did what I had to do and now here I am surrounded by all these different women. Some are murderers, child molesters, drug dealers and addicts, gang bangers, scammers, bank robbers, etc.... Hard-core criminals, including myself. But only God can judge us.

I can't speak for anyone but myself. Without a doubt I accept full responsibility of the consequences from the lifestyle I choose. I'm writing to you today as a living testament, prayer changed things. Since I've been incarcerated I have reconnected with my higher power. I accomplished getting my GED. I'm writing my first book, but most importantly I have learned how to be flexible mentally. I practice humility daily. I have found myself and my peace of mind. Going or coming to prison can be bad or good. It's all on how you apply yourself. I look at it like this: "God puts us in places where we don't want to be, to get us to where he needs us to be."

First, I want to thank God. Then, I want to say thanks to Patrice for the opportunity to share my story. To my dear mother, I love you. Shout out to my brother Jean and my sister, Liline. I dedicate this to everyone that had my back my whole bid. Shout out to the few sincere people I met while going through this dark time of my life. Shout out to Nay, Quae, Ked, Sophie. I love you all so much!

    Jessica Dorne
    #14083-104

May 30th, 2018

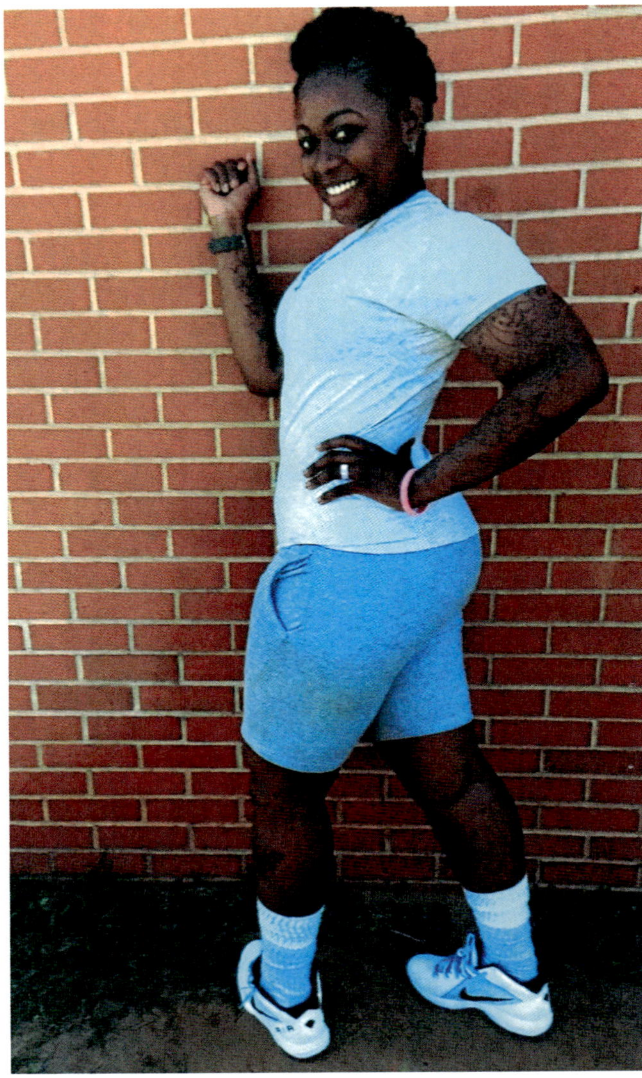

RICH IN SPIRIT

Kisha E. Singletary

It's crazy how when you're in the process of getting your life together after a storm in your life, a whole tornado comes. That's sort of what occurred around the time I got caught up in this ten-year bid I'm serving.

My name is Kisha Ericka Singletary. I'm twenty-five years old. Before this incarceration lifestyle I'm living in, I was enrolled at Miami-Dade College getting ready to become an R.N. I also was doing part-time security jobs and hustling hard on the side. I came from nothing and grew up with enough, but less than others. You already know when I jumped off the porch I hit the ground running. My grind to the top was non-stop. I had no guidance, no parents to help me move wiser, and better, than I was. That alone played a huge factor in my demise. There really wasn't no limit to the things I did to make sure I was good. All in all I was it, or at least, I thought I was. Until I started to get way too big for my britches. I was moving real sloppy and reckless, like I was untouchable. God came through and brought me down a notch.

Everything went left the day I got robbed twice in one day and in the process of getting robbed I got arrested for this federal warrant pertaining to this federal case I'm now getting over with. Coming from the city of Miami, shit gets real, like that, and you gotta do what you gotta do to survive. I learned a lot from this experience. I learned people really ain't your people—outta sight, outta mind—and you really find out who folks is when you're down and out. I also got close to God and gained that personal relationship He so desperately wanted. I'm blessed, I was blind but now I see the bigger picture and a clearer goal and a better way to reach it. I'm ready. I got this, watch me turn a negative situation into a positive, blessed outcome. God is Love and He will never put more on you than you can bear. Always remember if you put your trust in man, he will fail you every time but if you put your trust in God He will never let you down. Amen.

Love, a poor little rich girl.

Kisha E. Singletary
#06635-104

07/28/2018 19 38

1 WAY 2 LIVE 2 NO WAY OUT

Mallori "Bunny" Moss

My name is Mallori Moss, although most people know me as Bonnie or Bunny. My name was given to me through my life of crime. Which brought me to this point in my life, being held in federal prison on conspiracy to commit bank fraud and aggravated identity theft.

Really it all started when I was very young. I committed my first crimes at the age 10, stealing to get clothes for school and the things I wanted. My mother did her best, she worked hard and tried to show me as much love as she knew how to at the time but I love her with all my heart.

I left the house at an early age of fourteen, running around partying, hanging out and selling drugs to survive. Really anything had a price except for myself. I struggled through my teen years to keep my head above water. I ended up pregnant at fifteen with my first child, Ryan. I did my best but I wasn't prepared mentally to raise a child. I had extreme postpartum depression and my mother picked up my slack. She didn't have much herself, just a deadbeat boyfriend who was abusive to me and to her in different ways. He ended up leaving her with nothing but a wet ass and a child who is my sister. I continued to do what I had to do. Selling drugs to take care of not just myself but also those around me and the household.

I ended up meeting this man who was ten years older than me. I thought he was my knight in shiny armor and would save me from the life I was living. He promised everything, and being naive, I believed into all his lies.

I ended up pregnant with my second child, Chanel. I thought everything was going to be okay now. He had thousands saved up and a house in the suburbs, only to find out quickly that he lied about the money and the house was his cousin's and they got evicted; I'm pregnant and I thought I was in love. I thought because he was ten years older than me, he had hisself together and could give me the direction I needed and sweep me off my feet. He was a dope boy and once Chanel came into the world everything changed.

He started cheating on me, not coming home. I fought the whole hood twice behind this man. Me being the independent person I am I started taking over his lil operation and making all the money sitting on the block. While he stayed home, smoked weed and sat on his ass. I felt trapped, only risking my freedom to sell drugs to take care of not only my new family but also help those I loved, too. This went on for almost five years. I worked in strip clubs, sold drugs, took care of my daughter and the house, while he did what he wanted to do.

Then one day I got pulled over and got caught with some drugs and arrested. I was put on drug court probation and of course I continued my lifestyle. Which eventually led me right back to jail. I now sat with no bond, no way of getting out and no one to talk to. My daughter Chanel was now three and my son Ryan, seven. I have never been away from Chanel for no more than a few hours even living the way I was. I think this was the most traumatic experience for me. Not the sexual abuse, or emotional abuse or growing up with the bare minimum; no, it was being locked up and away from those I loved.

THE COURAGE TO SOAR BEHIND BARS

Well, doing this time I ended up getting one hundred eighty days in county, nothing too serious. During this time Chanel's father, the man I thought I loved and endured all with, left me in jail, took off with Chanel and got married to a woman he was having an affair with. I got released from county and tried to find my little girl but he moved and would answer the phone and tell me to meet him places and never show up. The pain hurt so bad I felt powerless without her. I had no money, nothing but clothes on my back. I had to survive so I went head first in the streets, got a front and began doing what I knew to do best.

I ended up starting to pop Percocet and hydrocodone to numb the feelings I felt from losing the only thing that kept me motivated and sane. My mother was raising my son, Ryan, and she loved him as her own. I had so much weight on my shoulders from trying to make ends meet. I was living at my smokers' (dope fiends) houses and renting their vehicles. I would be on the block all day and night or working off my phone. I was the only female. I've never really trusted women. I guess because all the women closer to me in my life betrayed me to a point I trusted none of them. So, I always surrounded myself with men.

Anyways, well my mother was in a rat- and roach-infested house trying to make ends meet with my son. My sister, my cousin and my uncle, all who looked to me at some point in their life. I've always been the independent one and everyone always looked to me for what was next. I tried my best to take care of me and to help my family as well. But po' hustling on the block wasn't cutting it. I would never get off the corners. I needed to make a change.

Well that changed happened...One of my friends who I loved a lot, who taught me a lot about life, the streets, the game and the codes, his name was Lashawn, we used to be on the block together. We ended up getting locked up with a high bond. Of course me being the rider and loyal person I am, I did whatever to get the money to get him out. I would pop XOs (ecstasy) to stay up for days at a time to be on the block, so I wouldn't miss a dollar. One night I even got robbed by three men and got two teeth knocked out, but not before I stabbed one of them; that didn't stop me.

One day I was at the carwash in Daytona and I met a man whose name was P. He was tall and stalky, with gold in his mouth on every tooth. He asked me if I wanted to make some money. I was leery and hesitant but due to my circumstances and now my best friend lock up, I was willing to take a chance. So I listened to what him and the other "check boys" had to say. I agreed and went to work for one day. My intention was only to work for one day because, be honest, I was a "Dope Girl" and that's all I knew and felt comfortable doing.

This bank shit was out of my lane. So I got me two grand at the end of the day. That was enough for me to come up, put some money on my friend's (Lashawn) bond and re-up. Well, he insisted I come one more time. So that was the first day of a whole new life…That day there was a police chase, we managed to escape but instead of me going back to the block he took me with him all the way to his city, Fort Lauderdale.

I ended up paying my friend's bond through the phone but it would be a while before he saw my face again. P took me to Fort Lauderdale, took me shopping and put me in a motel. I started to pay attention to all the men around me and all the activities. I played like I was slow but all the while I was learning a whole new hustle. I was now in a position to make thousands of dollars. I sat back and watched, I seen all the money that came in and then noticed how much I was given…which was peanuts. I thought to myself since that I was going to play my position to the best, until I obtained the knowledge I needed to leave from around them. I ended up using my sexuality to get into P's head.

He ended up like I expected, weak for pussy, telling me everything I needed to know. About two months later, me, him and four other men packed up in different rental cars with black-tinted windows. I was directed to follow the car ahead of me, with distance between us on the highway. So we didn't attract attention from the Feds and state troopers on the highway. I had no idea where I was headed or to what state but I had nothing to lose and everything to gain. I was lost trying to find myself. Trying to figure out what to do at this point; I was wanted already. I had a warrant issued from that chase that I was in before leaving Daytona.

So going back there was not an option until I had the money to get me out of the shit I was in. I used to call Chanel's dad but he'd never answer and when he did he'd want to talk about me fucking him and if I fuck him he'd let me see our daughter, but he was a liar. I tried that once and he came alone so I never fell into that trap again.

Well, after driving almost twenty-four hours we finally stop in Dallas, Texas, the final destination. This would soon be my new home. Little did I know, well P started putting his hands on me and threatening me. He became very jealous when we were around a lot of men and they'd always hit on me, but it wasn't about him. I was in it for the money, only.

My goal was to save up thousands of dollars, send to my mom and get things right so I could live comfortably. I started to notice a lot of betrayal going on in the crew. I was with a lot of sneaky things and plus a lot of them were very reckless and attracted too much attention for me. I knew this was a sinking ship so I immediately devised a plan. To get as far away from them as possible before I ended up drowning with them.

Not only that, I started getting this feeling that P was working with the Feds. Something he did was alarming, so first chance I got, I left them, took some money, got a room by myself and started getting money with someone else. I can go on and on about different high-speed chases and all the different men I was around and got money with.

This is around the time I recreated myself. I was no longer the poor girl who hustled on the back to make ends meet. I now had the knowledge to bring in thousands and thousands of dollars a day. I was making so much money, I didn't know what to do with it. Most of the time I would give it away to the boys on the block trying to make theirs, and buy kids in the hood shoes, clothes, and the rest, blow it on strippers. I ended up meeting people in Texas and started introducing them to my lifestyle.

I was now in top position and worked my way up. Although, I was still lonely, I still had an emptiness. I used to pop perks all day and night. I became reliant on them. I committed felony and federal offenses daily. I ended up getting a nice house in the suburbs, flying my mother up to Dallas and having her get money with me, so she could have it to take back to Florida. I felt like I was on top of the world, like I was untouchable. I had a crew of people around me that loved and respected me as I did them.

We all took what we did serious and we all made sure we ate. It was The Life but all good things come to an end and karma always come around…I got a phone call from this man I used to get all my rental cars from. He said the Feds was shopping around, asking questions about his involvement in "The Felony Lane Gang" (this is the name the Feds gave to all of us.) I felt my heart drop into my stomach.

The good times was about to be over. I acted nonchalant and agreed to have the vehicles turned in, I didn't want any trouble coming to those who were clueless. I called up my homeboy, my best friend, "bruh bruh," cuz he was just that to me, like a brother. I told him to catch a flight and go home, shit's about to get real. I ordered him to turn his car in. We argued and he was reluctant but he did what I said. It broke my heart to tell him to leave, he was my right hand through this time, but I only wanted to protect him. So we got into an argument and I dropped him off.

Never to see him again in the free world. See, I just found out that I was pregnant with my third child. I had no intention of having another baby. I was on federal radar and bond for numerous evading arrests and fraud charges. And plus the guilt of me not being there for my children...it caused me to start thinking of getting an abortion. Something I never wanted but God had different plans for me and my life. Three days after I told my home boy to leave, the Feds and the state came to my house, arrested everyone in it including me, my workers, my mother and my boyfriend at the time...I had a $100,000 dollar bond.

I lost everything: my money and the house, my furniture and EVERYTHING! I did have a lawyer retained. The best advice I can give to anyone, living a life by the Law! My bond was posted and I was released within that week. The feds didn't have enough on me to keep me...so they were not happy. They wanted me "behind bars" and definitely I got and lost everything but within two days I was good again. I started getting money, everyone looked at me like, "What's next?"

I obtained another house, started saving money and preparing to do some lil county time. I had ten felonies through Texas and I had the top lawyer in Dallas but I still knew, I would have to sit for a few months. I did what I had to do to save up for when I was gone. My boyfriend would be straight and he would be able to take care of everything while I was gone—so I thought...?

   I only knew him about three months, all I did for him, his family and children. I just knew he'll be my backbone, and I was pregnant. On January 27, 2014 I was walking in the mall shopping to get me something to wear to the club that night like I did every night and an officer noticed me. I was out on a $100,000-dollar bond but I ended up wanted in three counties within three weeks of being released. So when I noticed the officer walking towards me, I did what I never do...I surrendered. He made me sit down on the floor and immediately choked me because I'm well known for going on pursuit any way I can, on foot or in the car. I sat there, two months pregnant, on the floor in the mall, threw my keys to my boyfriend and told him "This is it!"

I loved him and I knew I'll see him in a few months. I was locked up, held with no bond and wanted in three different counties. My lawyer couldn't get me out if he wanted to. This was the end of my road. I wasn't the least bit worried. I had thousands in cash, my car, a lawyer already paid and all my homeboys were safe back in Fort Lauderdale. To my knowledge all I had to do is my time and I'd be free in like six months. My lawyer got me a deal with all I had and owned. That's all I needed. I thought...

I had much trust issues and from seeing all I've seen in my life, I grew to be paranoid, not trusting many. So no one knew my government name, they knew me by "Bunny," but it's all good. I had my man and he loved me, he had my back. This was a lesson for me I'll never forget. Never put all your eggs in one basket, and you can't buy love-n-loyalty. It's either in you or it's not...and most people don't have your best interest at heart.

I was locked up not even seven days and my boyfriend, soon to be my child's father, took everything from me, all my money, cars and jewelry. Never answered the phone and left me in jail pregnant and alone. I had access to no one, only my lawyer. I had no one's number and only a handful knew my real name. I was broke, had no money on my account. I went from making thousands of dollars and having everything I wanted, to having nothing, no soap, no hygiene, nothing! I was devastated...I was halfway across the country from where I grew up. I was lost and scared. I didn't know what would happen with my baby once I had her. All I could do is pray. So that's what I did, I got on my knees and prayed for the strength to endure all I had in front of me.

I would talk to God and my unborn child every day and prayed for her to be taken care of. Well, my boyfriend's mother, whom I loved very much, was there for me. Her and her boyfriend assured me that they would be there to pick up my little girl, who I named Ca-lyiah, and that's just what they did. June 13, 2014, she was a beautiful eight pounds, twelve ounces when I had her in Tarrant County. I got sentenced two weeks after I had her, to eight months state jail with my back time I've served. I would be home by September 2014. Going home and committing crimes was not an option. I wanted to raise my little girl and be a mommy, not a "Dope Girl" or "Check Girl," a finesser. Just a normal mom. Get a job, go to school and live simple.

I got my release date; it was September 21, 2014. I felt free…I had less than a month left. I was in state prison in Texas and the conditions were unbearable, no a/c, one hundred twenty degree weather, it was truly hell on earth.

Well, my whole world came crashing down on me again…Karma's a Bitch! Let me tell you! All the money I made. All the crimes I committed…weeks before I was to be released, the Feds indicted me on bank conspiracy and aggravated identity theft.

The news had me emotional and exhausted. I felt heart-broken and mad. I just wanted to get out and live normal. Now another one of my children would be raised by someone other than me and I'd be gone definitely for years! I never spoke to anyone about my case or crimes or the life I lived, when I was in county and state prison because I knew the Feds were watching and I was trying to slip through the cracks. My home boy "bruh bruh" even reached out to me one time when I was in the county and I told him to stay far away from me. I knew the Feds was lurking around and they finally got me!

I was transferred to the federal holding within the week where I seen my mom (mother) my workers, Kat Stacks, and a number of men who I've met through the years of my "check game." I had sixteen people on my indictment. My mom, my boyfriend who left me for dead, my workers, and it broke my heart, "bruh bruh" plus others. I've ran across some I knew well, others I didn't know. Everyone started turning on each other on the indictment. I remained silent and solid because I knew this day would come and this is part of the game, the life I was living. I had a hard time in holding. I was very angry.

Not being able to raise my little girl, Ca-lyiah. And all the people who I showed love to turned their backs on me, even my own mother. I was in solitary behind the door for most of my time in holding but through those lonely nights and hard times, I grew in ways I can't explain.

But through all my experiences I regret nothing. You live and you learn. Writing my story and telling of me has been inspirational and therapeutic for me. It allowed me to look back, reflect and to see what really matters in life. To Ryan, Chanel, Ca-lyiah, my mother, "Wendi," and to my best friend, bruh bruh, aka Me Me, y'all has been my hope and strength when times I felt like giving up. Love never ends and love endures all things.

Love,

Mallori "Bunny" Moss
#22667-078

03/11/2018 11:39

ORDER OUT OF CHAOS

Tetria N. Hill

My name is Tetria Nicole Hill. I was born September 18, 1981 in a small town in Alabama called Brewton. My mother was divorced with four children. We moved to Pensacola, FL when I was eight months. I have three brothers and a sister who really love and care for me.

We didn't have much growing up, but we had each other. My mom was hospitalized when I was thirteen because of her heart condition. What was supposed to be a minor outpatient procedure turned into a triple bypass surgery and a six-month hospital stay for her. Not really planning to be away that long put me and my siblings in a bad place. My sister and I went to stay with my grandmother and aunts. Two months later I was acting out, homesick, and wanting to see my mom and brothers. I begged to go back to Florida and stay with my mom's best friend and one of my godmothers, Brenda, with my brothers. My brothers were already in the streets. Watching how they moved made me want to get some money, the transactions seemed pretty easy. Plus my mind was made up that I never wanted my mom to work or struggle ever again.

By the time I was sixteen I was buying a pound of weed a week to sell. As long as I was going to school and not getting into trouble no one seemed to mind my mischief. When I was seventeen my mom got me a job at a call center making good money plus commission. At least now I could help pay the bills and help stay out of the streets and not stress my mom. With this job my grades started to slip and when it was time to graduate I was informed I was four credits short and I couldn't walk with my class, so I said forget it and started hanging out heavy.

I was smoking weed more and started to drink more. I got pregnant at nineteen with my son, Trejon, again at twenty-one with my daughter, Breyon, and again at twenty-three with my son, Tabious. Now I'm a single mother of three beautiful kids whom I adore and want to give the world.

I decided to go back to school and get my G.E.D. I passed it on my first try and decided to continue my education and go to college for Health Information Management. While I was enrolled in school I was presented with an opportunity to make some money so I could catch up on my bills and give my kids the things they want. Of course I was down. A while later I was pulled over in Beaumont, Texas with six kilos of cocaine. The Feds picked up my case and I was sentenced to one hundred twenty months as a first-time felon.

So now I sit here in prison. My kids are getting older and I can't give them anything but distant love and advice. My mom, family, and friends have stood by me through this whole ordeal. I spend my time praying and programming. While I was in a nine-month residential drug abuse program I learned my struggles with my criminal thinking and how to overcome them by challenging my thoughts and using positive self-talk. As I reenter back into society I would like to dedicate some of my time to young ladies and make them aware of their choices and empower them to be more than just pawns in this life we are living. Also, I'm going to make up for lost time I have spent away from my kids and be the best mom God put me on the earth to be!

    Tetria N. Hill
        #23450-017

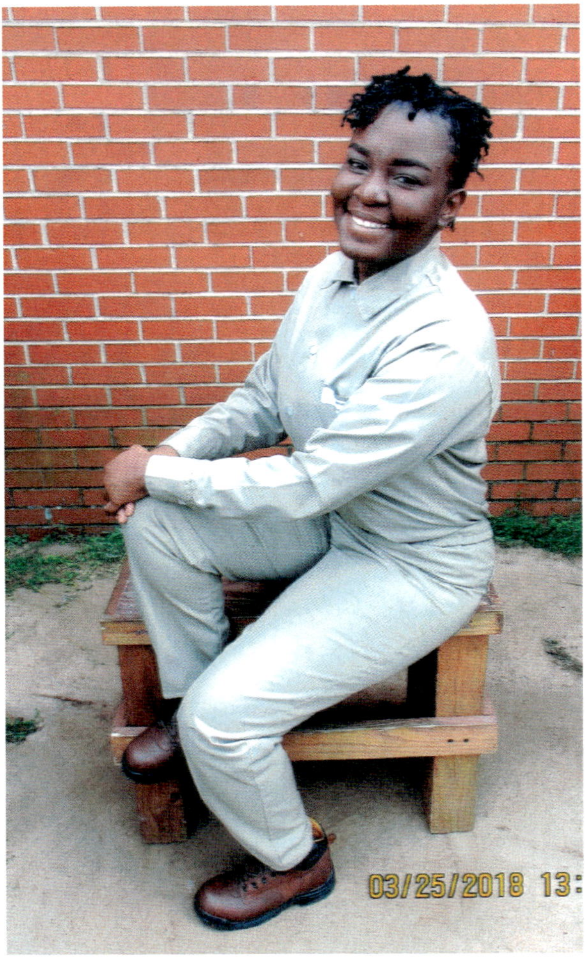
03/25/2018 13:

DREAMS WORTH MORE THAN MONEY

Jerrisha "Risha" Rawlins ("CoCo")

    I sat in my room in Guaynabo, Puerto Rico, wondering, "How did I even end up here?" I pointed fingers, blaming my home, St. Thomas, of the U.S. Virgin Islands. There, it's all about survival, it's about who you know and who knows you, and because it's so small everyone knows everything about everyone else. That being said, when I got arrested, the news of my arrest spread like a wildfire across my island before the day's end.

    My name is Jerrisha Rawlins—Risha for short—but to those here at FCI Tallahassee, I'm CoCo. Twenty-three years old and the baby of my family, I am a first-time offender and the first of my family to become a felon–not exactly what you would call an accomplishment. I grew up with dreams of maybe being a singer or even a rapper. I remember as a kid, when I would perform my favorite songs to my stuffed animals. As I grew older I fell in love with hip-hop. Unlike the other kids who enjoyed the sweet sounds of Calypso and Soca, I was a "rap-head" and I have my brother Jerry to thank for that.

He would always have his stereo blasting all kinds of hip-hop and he and I would always jam together. My favorite group was Outkast and, of course, my favorite rappers were Lil Wayne and Eminem. Then, I had goals. I had always dreamed of laying down tracks with Lil Wayne and even becoming a music producer or song writer myself one day. The older I got, however, the more I doubted myself and my dreams. Big mistake.

By the time I was a freshman in high school, I was smoking weed and drinking liquor.

I had no ambition—I only wanted to drink, party, and let myself waste away. Graduate from high school? Nope, I dropped out. I didn't care about my education but others always saw something in me that, for a long time, I didn't see in myself. At the age of 16, I met a guy named Jordan who would become my greatest friend. He showed me how to do graphic design, and in all honesty, he helped me to rebuild my ambition. As a producer himself, he showed me many tools of the trade and I was around him 24/7 before he moved to Orlando. By that time, both my love for music and my ambition were restored and no one could deter me from my goals.

At the age of twenty I, too, moved to Orlando to pursue my dreams, with no direction, diploma, or even a clear-out plan. I was still able to find and manage my first artist and soon, I begin to envision myself opening my own studio and putting my artist on the map. For a moment, life in Orlando was great, but as fate would have it, my life took a turn when I had lost my job in 2016.

After five months, the financial strain of being unemployed started to weigh heavily on me. At this point, I got an offer to clean drug money and, like we say back home, "From the first pump of the spray bottle," I was in. Seeing all of that money in front of me was like a high, and I knew, if I stuck around long enough, that I would be able to open my studio or at least get my artist a feature with a popular artist.

As time went on, I had gone on numerous trips with the woman who was like my supervisor. I didn't know it at the time, but she would have cocaine secretly stashed. Something within me would always set off red flags, but I was so naive then, that I had ignored the signs. All I could see was the money, not the path I was headed down. By week three, I was able to clean and pack drug money without supervision—and even smoke a joint afterwards. I was even a little street smart, you couldn't catch me flossing bands or talking business over the phone. My supervisor, however, was not so savvy.

I wanted to throw her phone in the nearest lake at times. I always had a feeling that things would go South but my mindset ended up becoming "Fuck it. I ain't stoppin' till they come knockin'."

June 20, 2016

I did something that I never saw myself doing—I did something without any knowledge of even having done it in the first place: I pushed cocaine through St. Thomas airport. It all started when my supervisor took my cousin and me to Colorado. We were excited, but my stomach felt uneasy for some reason. As usual, I ignored this feeling and looked forward to smoking Kush in Colorado. When we laid by the pool at the hotel that night, just me and the supervisor, she turned to me and said, "You know what was in your bag today?"

Puzzled, I replied, "Money."

I remember how she laughed at me before saying "I'm glad I didn't tell you ahead of time, you probably would of bucked on me."

I was stunned by her comment, and I had realized she smuggled cocaine in my bag and played with My Life. Why didn't I stop then? In a way, I felt like I was my own Boss. I called my own shots and lust for money overrode my better judgement...

July 2016

The first arrest happened. My other codefendants and

I had told the girl to not make the trip. We all felt something deep within our souls, telling us not to, and clearly, she didn't listen to her own intuition. They were waiting for her at the airport when it all happened.

I was arrested four months after my twenty-second birthday. I knew it would all happen sooner or later. I was a rebel for a moment though. I argued with the Feds about my role until I almost became blue in the face. The DA finally got it through my head that I was only playing with my own life if I kept being stubborn. I admitted to my own role—now it was just a waiting game. I had to sit in the same unit with the woman who told on me. My only goal in mind at that point was to get my G.E.D—after all, that was the thing that the judge kept throwing in my face. The way he put me down for not having my H.S. diploma. I refused to just sit and do nothing with My Life.

I would listen to Meek Mill and be inspired and reminded to never give up on my dreams. Now, I use my current situation to motivate me to push myself harder. When I hit FCI Tallahassee in December 2017, I was enrolled by February 2018 and I tested out and got my G.E.D. by March 2018. In June 2018, I enrolled in Culinary Arts VT and became certified in September 2018. I participated in the Residential Drug Abuse Programs (RDAP) and over time, I rebuilt myself. I refuse to come back here, I refuse to let my dreams slip through my hands, again...

To all the young men and women in my generation who are in prison, "take a look at yourself." Are you proud of the person you've become? Are those "friends" still around? While you sit on time, what are you doing to make yourself better? You are not alone; this is the last place I expected to be. This is not the last resort. I've been broken down mentally over and over. Don't let the system swallow you. Don't give up on yourself, because that's what they want.

You can learn in this environment and when someone sees something in you, believe it! I've met so many women in here, I learn from them.

I gained so much knowledge just by talking to them and also I've met women who believed in my dream, who believe I got what it takes and I'm grateful to experience this. It's not where I wanna be but this is where God needed me, he had to sit me down so I can see that I was gonna lose myself, the streets was going to take over my life and I was blinded to my dreams, but now I'm leaving as a different person than the one who got arrested in Orlando two or three years ago.

I'm content with myself, and with every setback, there's a major comeback. I will be enrolling in college to get my goals, aka my dreams, started. This is just a stepping stone…

"Who Jah Bless, No man curse."
Keep your head leveled!

Jerrisha "Risha" Rawlins ("CoCo"), St. Thomas, USVI

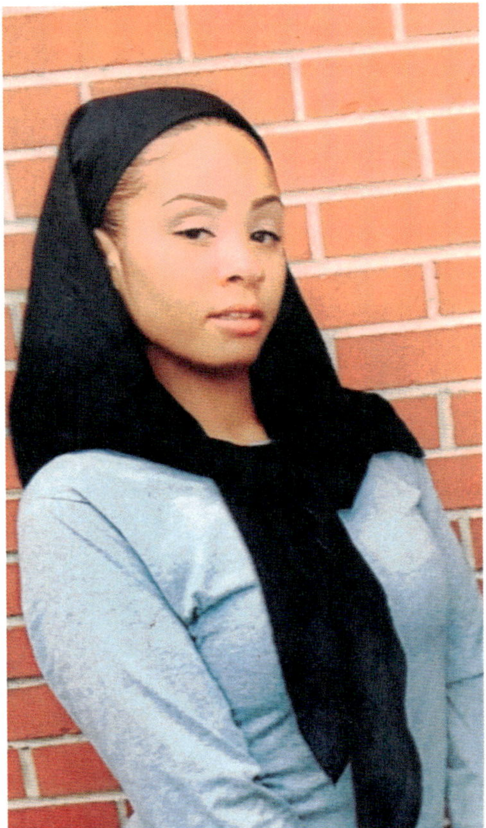

LETTER TO MY CLYDE

Mona' Li

Skin so smooth, milk chocolaty painted;
Body covered in ink so beautifully tainted.
Damn he's fine, so fine, too fine.
Flipped me, split me and fucked my mind.
False confession of a love got me caught in a trance;
And I don't even know that he's someone else's man.
Another one night stand so I thought as I left;
Yet two days later we were covered in sweat.
Wining me and dining me and sexin' me good;
Chivalry is dead? Yea, well not in the hood.
Everything I wanted and nothing I needed;
A craving like no other, I utterly fiend it.
You wanna do what? Yeah sure, not a problem;
Thirty days later it was banks we were robbin'.
His Bonnie, My Clyde, What a crazy thought;
And he said he'd take the fall if we ever got caught.
Bullet-proof plans don't have loose ends;
Cold feet saved the nigga that called us in.

You lost the money, not me. Why you trippin'?

And the pig that pulled you over…safe to say he was slippin'.

Left me in a tellie, man paranoia ran deep;

Puffed some loud, downed some Quil, shit and still couldn't sleep.

Did I mention it's my birthday? What a lovely surprise;

Next day I was up, dressed and ready to ride.

Down for whatever, damn. I just wanted you near;

Flashbacks of daddy's suicide fueling this fear.

Wells Fargo…What's that saying? Oh…Together we'll go far

As they foreclosed my mama's house in 2010, leaving scars!?

My bad…Where was I? Ahh, ok, here we go again;

A simple head nod to set it off. Allah forgive me for my sins.

Quick money, fast money, straight money, no chaser;

You had a good girl, yet so determined to change her.

Terror filled her chest, I can see her running through the house;

She was a stupid little girl with dreams of being ya spouse.

You loved her, loved to choke her, picked her up, knocked her down;

Whispered threats to take her life and leave her body unfound;

If she never faked that pregnancy, she probably wouldn't be 'round;

Plus the help of being hemmed up and cuffed on the ground.

You have the right to "blah, blah, blah" you've seen all

the shows;

Cooped up in a holdin' cell with petty thieves and cheap hoes;

Stripped of everything, "squat," "cough," left fully exposed;

Along with dirty little secrets of the man that I chose.

Yea, the Feds gave me the tea about affairs and ya lovers;

It was then they spilled the beans about you fuckin' ya "brother";

And something of a troubled past and a crackhead mother;

Looking back it's clear to see that you were lustin' another.

Thoughts of disease and HIV and never using a rubber;

All praise to God if it's been His will that I not bear that struggle;

As my mom cries tears of joy that I'm still here to hug her;

Caught this case, she raised my son, for that I'll always love her;

Mentally you broke me down and yet you showed me my worth;

Today I understand the value of what's under my skirt;

Physical scars, visible memories, no longer hurt;

Mentally I got back up and dusted off that dirt.

I'm smarter now, I'm stronger now, so I could never hate you;

For the abuse and isolation I just wanna thank you;

As I make du'a on your behalf that there's still time to save you;

And that Shaytaan fall short in mission while he try to astray you.

No longer yours, Bonnie

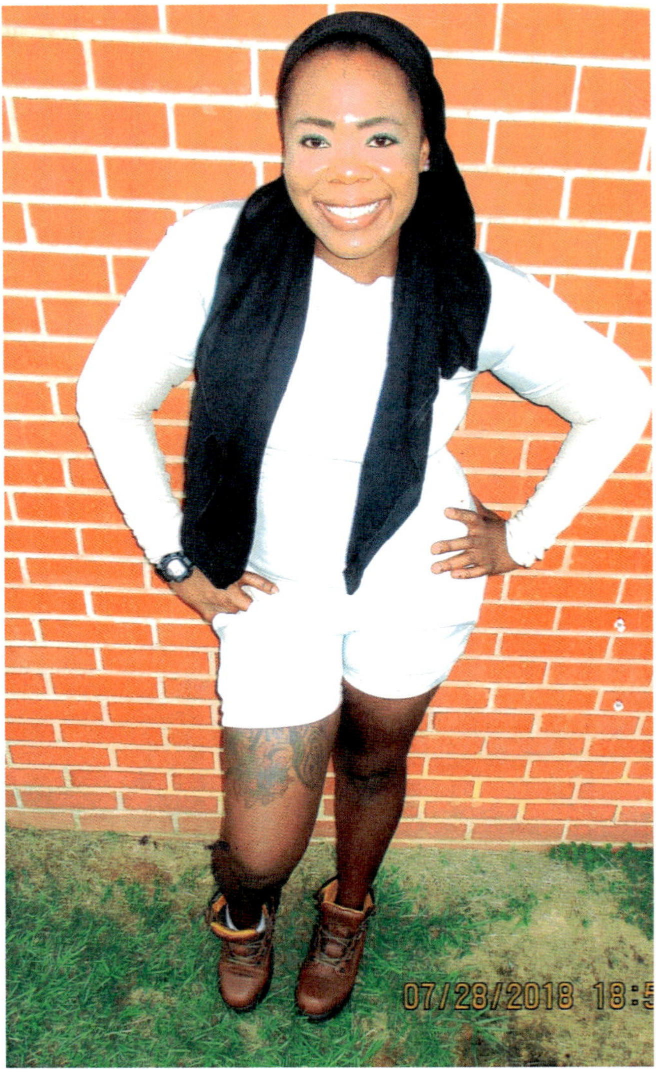
07/28/2018 18:5

CLUB PARADISE

Sandra Simon

My name is Sandra Simon, aka Solo by the streets and the Feds. I was federally indicted at 23, when most are either graduating college or happily married or popping out babies. I was facing life for the second time in less than two years. How did my life come to this, Sandra Simon versus the United States?

I grew up in a household of ten, me, my seven other siblings, my mom and dad. My dad left when I was one, leaving my mom to fend for herself and her eight children. Even though only three of us was his, my baby brother and older sister. She had it tough raising us, Section 8 and food stamps, jobs here and there. It was hard to have what the other kids had. So growing up, always wanting what wasn't available, made me $$$ (money) hungry.

Fights and dropping out of school seemed to be a major recurrence in my city. Shootouts in my middle school was nothing too far from the ordinary. Me and my friends always wanted the best, we lived in Waterstone, one of the best gated communities in the Miami Southern District. But there was nothing Section 8 couldn't pay, but when you're living around other snotty-nose kids who really got it, but your parents don't, you think of your options.

So we started skipping school and shoplifting for the nicest hair, clothes, shoes, jewelry—at thirteen we was lit. The best dressed in the school, I guess now the wardrobe matched the house. But then the haters came and so did the fights, getting kicked to opportunity school where I later dropped out of the 8th grade, signed up for Medical School, which took me all the way up to studying cardiology.

I was seventeen on this dating website, just for fun, and of course, I never lied about my age. I've always seemed to attract the older crowd though, but of course, I was shy at first. But after losing this mini job I had at sixteen for trying to steal a customer's credit card number and getting caught, I still had bills and wants, so I started hanging out with the weirdos who wanted this young chick by their side (me) making between three hundred to five hundred daily. By the end of the week, I had racks (thousands) easily, of course.

My family had questions to where I was getting this money. I lied and said well, my boyfriend gave it to me. But of course there was no boyfriends (lol), just toy friends.

School was starting and one day my home girl (Roseline) called me up wanting to borrow some money to buy all her new school stuff. We were the same age; my birthday literally one day before hers...I explained to her, well, there's this guy who I'm no longer interested in and I really need him to stop blowing up my phone; he has money, but just not enough to my liking. His name is Raymond.

He was twenty-eight and black, nice car, nice job, but he was just such a bug. So I gave her his number and later texted him, telling him it wouldn't work out, but he's a nice person for you. I later explained to her after giving her his number, saying he will take you shopping. Just make sure you get me something cute. But of course, like every snake female that I've came to know, she redlined, with me ending that friendship.

But there is something I've noticed in me, that I can help others, helping me help myself. I was "Madam Ready." I continued my hoeing for the years to come, taking trips to Orlando, Ritz Carlton resorts, Four Seasons, Fontainebleau, South Beach and Sunny Isles Condominiums. Trips back and forth to California. I was in high demand even with the pimps out of state, every John in Miami knew me, every hoe wanted to work with me, and every pimp wanted to own me! But I was Solo, choosing my company very wisely, only to become foolish for the one man I've always had a soft spot for: my co-defendant, "Jermaine."

I've always been a renegade, but for him I made exception. I never called him daddy, or claimed him as my pimp. He was my best friend, and me, his; he had his baby mamas and his hoes and I had my tricks! I upgraded him and he upgraded me, you couldn't even speak foul about me around him, or you will be slapped down. His family loved me. Just to one day hate me, but their opinion about me didn't even matter, even to the point he went against everybody. The world defending me on all grounds.

We had a couple females I trained on his behalf, always checking, making sure everyone was over age, to the point I started trusting him completely. I knew his family, he knew mine. One night he called and said he need me to get with two females he has. He explained they were nineteen, and he needed me to teach them them the ropes. I agreed to do it on his behalf.

Two hours later, we were all at the hotel. I met them, one looked similar to the rapper Iggy Azalea and the other looked like Miley Cyrus. I introduced myself and so did they. They both told me they were nineteen, even before I asked. But after seventy-two hours with these females it was clear they were other. Their way of thinking was just a little too blonde, although they were blonde. They just didn't seem mature enough to be nineteen.

I asked again very maturely and seriously, "Listen, how

old are you guys, I promise to not trip."

They replied separately, "I'm fifteen," "I'm sixteen," and then they stated Jermaine said to tell you we were nineteen. I couldn't believe it! I grabbed myself and called Jermaine, explaining the type of time that carried, putting people with their age in this kind of business. Heavily upset that somebody I knew would blatantly lie to me and put me in danger for the simple greed of money.

I hung up, grabbed my belongings, telling the girls I would be back, "I'm going to go get cigarettes," and I never returned. A month later, the federal agents were looking for me. I ran for two weeks, and eventually got caught when an undercover cop from Miami-Dade set up a date just to bust me, to have a reason to speak to me. The same detective from "First 48: Miami Homicide." The crazy part about it was I was watching the "First 48" when he came in and busted me with the other federal agents pointing guns at me in my face. They interviewed me; of course, I knew they had no case. I denied any involvement, claiming me and Jermaine's innocence. The detective stated at the end of the interview, "But mark my word, you will be indicted facing life."

Three months later the U.S. Marshalls picked me up from Miami County Jail and I was arraigned and charged with sex trafficking of a minor (two counts) and sex trafficking of a minor (conspiracy, one count). Ten years minimum mandatory to life.

My arraignment was on Christmas Eve of 2014. I pleaded guilty April 29, 2015, on my twenty-fourth birthday and was sentenced to eleven years and four months and ten years probation. My co-defendant was sentenced to thirty-two years after losing at trial, appealed, but denied a year later.

The Moral of the story is when you trust nobody, you're only protecting yourself. The ones you love will be the ones to hurt you in the end. The fast life comes with a price, your life, at the end of the day. No price or nobody is worth your Freedom.

They call me Solo. If I would have followed that motto, I wouldn't be here, though, story of my life—at least 5% of it. To be continued…

Sandra Simon
    #07208-104

01/12/2018 19:35

SAABIR THE GREAT

Jaqualah Banks

To: The World
From: Badazz a.k.a Bandana a.k.a Yolo Bangs a.k.a Saabir the Great
Mood: G-Mackin on my sly fox
Place: Federal Pen
Song: Mind Frame—Money Bagg Yo

Waz Gucci, Louie, Prada this that nigga Qua a.k.a G-Baby as they know of me behind the G-wall. I'm'a give the world a flash inside my "mind frame." I'm from Newark, New Jersey. "Brick City"—yes, yes that New Jersey drive city fast, cars, bitches, money, and so much more. I stay on the wave let's go get it, follow my speed, I got the sauce, I got the juice, I am now twenty-eight years old. I been doing time since I was nineteen years old. I am a F2M Transgender (female to male), I'm black, P.R. (Puerto Rican) and Cuban. I am a Muslim (Saabir Malik Abdul-

Haleem). Saab ir (patient) Malik (King) Abdul-Haleem (Patience of Allah), that's what my Muslim name means, and that is the name I'm living up to, and I must say I use to keep that "bag on me"; Crazy Life, Careless World, is how things are where I'm from.

In that world out there I was a good kid in a mad city, so I became a product of my environment and the money, drugs, cars, womans, and all the traveling caught me like a bug on a spider's web. I was a Dope Boy ballin, I had that "I don't give a ****" attitude. I loved guns, the grip around the handle was tight. I was into the rush, them streets ain't for no man so I had to keep my eyes on the snakes, these funny guys.

"Badazz" was with the shit, I got to the point I felt like it was my time to shine and I was shining so bright that the Feds saw me glowing and I ended up getting caught up like damn near everyone else; someone put the flash light on me, yeah, I was snatched on and I ended up with 180 months. I've been to Danbury, CT.; Hazelton, W.V.; Dublin, CA.; Aliceville, AL; Waseca, MN., and here I am at Tallahassee, FL. This is my sixth F.C.I. (Federal Correctional Institution). I've always been a fighter, never taking no mess. Doing time I must say isn't easy but God and my family has been rockin' with me from day one.

Now I gotta say, inside these walls I've learned patience, self-control; how to break out of habits and I know for a fact this isn't a place that I wouldn't dare come back to. I grew up doing all my twenties in Federal Prison. I have to say that I have TRULY COME a long way from the old self. It's levels to life, "I'm Blessed" because I still stand solid on all ten.

My life hasn't been glitter and gold, I was a wild boy

out on them streets. I'm not proud of my past but I was greedy for the cash, now I'm screamin' "Free The Real." I can't forget about transitioning female to male so that's a roller coaster in itself. I'm enjoying the effects of becoming a man but inside these walls I'm so misunderstood and they don't get my life; this is not my lifestyle, it's "Gay Pride." So every day I live like it's my last.

I've been through things inside these prison walls and out there in that world and I'm still on my journey. Words of Wisdom: "If you didn't go through the bad, you wouldn't know what the good was like."

    Jaqualah Banks
    #70497-056
        (056 is a North Carolina register # code)

05 12 2018

WHO AM I

Victorian L. Redwine

Who am I? That's the question most women behind bars ask themselves. I am one of these women. I found myself asking, "Who am I?" I'm a woman once bruised and battered by the things life threw at me.

At age fourteen I found myself taking care of myself. I was the little girl that was molested by men I trusted and once were close to my family. At age sixteen I was taking care of my sister who was fourteen. I worked and went to school. Age eighteen, I graduated with a 3.6 gpa. I should have went to college but I chose the streets. The streets chose me. I started using drugs and looking for love in all the wrong places. I was once lost but now I'm found. I have been through the storm and still going through it.

Now, at age twenty-eight I'm in federal prison, finding myself. I once told myself nothing was wrong with me but I see now that I am broken. I'm putting myself back together day by day. When I was younger I wanted to play in the WNBA. Those dreams were shattered, and becoming the next Queen Pin became a reality. It didn't last either. I'm blessed to have gotten a sentence of sixty months (five years) instead of one hundred twenty months (ten years). So I say all that to say I'm a survivor behind these barb wire fences.

I am smart, beautiful and intelligent. This khaki uniform doesn't define my character. #85356-380 doesn't define Who I Am. I am a woman of many words. I'm a woman who has overcome all the trials and tribulations life has to throw at someone. I am now the woman I thought never existed. I am a woman who empowers the women next to her to go above and beyond. I'm the woman that has overcame all the road blocks to change. I am a woman who isn't going back down the road I once traveled.

My name is Victorian L. Redwine and I am the woman who finally found herself. I'm going to continue to do what's right and make things better.

So I ask, do you know who you are behind these chained fences? "Let's Break every Chain!"

Victorian L. Redwine
#85356-380

03/25/2018 12:12

FROM HEELS TO MEDICAL SCHOOL

Denise Keaton

Good Day.

This tale of my life seems to be one that no one but I truly know. There are things I've never discussed and today I'm releasing some of those on paper but details are Vague.

To start by saying my childhood was bad would be a lie, to start off saying my childhood was great would be a lie, but to start off saying my childhood was in between the gray area would be spot on. My father went to prison before I was born so my early memories of him is current memories I'm making with my family. Institution Blue for him, Institution Khaki for me, are the only things that differ for the new and old memories, ten years of visitations, then my father came home to create new life when I turned thirteen. I think I'm skipping over details so let's rewind back to me.

Growing up, all I remember is prison visits, weekends with my godparents, living with my grandma, aunt or mom depending on the time line—you'll see it's been a back and forth type journey. I remember being in kindergarten or first grade, I attended Meadow Park Elementary School, and even though I literally stayed around the corner, I rode the bus to school. Well, one day I was on the bus and this big white boy, must have been in the fourth or fifth grade, was picking on me, bullying me, taking advantage of my size. Well, we got into a fight, yeah me (kindergarten/first grade) versus him (fourth or fifth grade). I didn't have any scratches but I fought for my life; I don't remember the outcome but I do remember emptying my piggy bank that had the pennies in it and giving him a bag of pennies.

I thought I could pay him to leave me alone. It must have worked because that was the last time he bothered me. What's amazing to me is how as adults we say kids don't know anything, but I've always been smart, gifted and exceptionally bossy (lol). Being the first girl among boy cousins, I fought the boys, played ball with boys, did everything the boys did, so girly stuff didn't come natural to me. I loved basketball, track but what's ironic is I was great at cheerleading and stepping.

Things from our past have a way of molding us into people. We have no clue who those people will become but I always knew what I wanted and how I could get it.

Fast forward from kindergarten and let's skip to fourth grade; throughout my life I've been bounced around and the same goes with schools. My fourth grade year I was at Powers Ferry Elementary in Marietta, Ga. I lived in Madison Garden near Dobbins Air Force base and there was a Circle K also in front of our complex.

My mother was a single parent with me and my brother whose father is also in prison. So when we came home we would go to our uncle's apartment or cousin's apartment since we were in the same complex. Well, when I would go outside I'd play with the neighborhood kids but we were ace boon coons: Landon, London, Chinasa, me and a few other girls, but the twins were my closest friends because we were all from Florida. There was this time when we went into the Circle K that we use to steal candy from and I was brave, this time I brought my Tinkerbell tote bag and I was ready. I had so much candy in this bag we just hauled ass out the door and ran through this cut behind the store that led us back to the complex and I end up stepping on a board with a nail on it. Well, well, well, that was my karma but it didn't stop me through my mischief. I never realized how little stealing candy was but it became a bigger habit.

I started boosting just because it was easy and not because I was making money. When I got to middle school it would be littler shit like socks, tote bags, CD's, pencils, stupid stuff, but in high school it was clothes, shoes, linen, and other stuff. I would do a grab and switch without leaving the store and it was lovely. The grab and switch is where I went in through the Gardening and grab a few water filters that were $70.00 apiece and get return stickers so I could go straight to the customer service desk to return them for gift cards that I'd later use for whatever. Clothes was even easier since I have this angelic look to me but I learned everyone has their kryptonite and a close friend of mine was that anytime we got together to hang out or steal we always got into trouble.

I later learned that she would be my downfall. I had no limit on what I would boost, if I could get it, I got it but it was always for self. I guess you could say my surroundings molded me, for some of the things I've done. My mother was a loving person, she had her share of ups and downs, but I wanted for nothing. I feel everything I did was because I could do it and not because I needed to do it. The things that led to my downfall were my goals and aspirations, but ultimately my mind and lack of patience. I could blame someone for this but it's ultimately my fault.

I've said it before and I'll say it again, I've always been smart, gifted and talented but patience wasn't on my side. My senior year in high school, I was accepted into a couple of colleges but the choice was between Florida A&M University and Alabama A&M University since HBCU was a must for me and cheerleading. I choose AAMU and this is where the rollercoaster began to descend. I tried out via video and made the team but before I could even see my first football game, I quit—not because I hated it or any reason you may think of but because I didn't have a way to get to campus for the first week of school so I made a decision that would alter the course of my life.

I called my coach and let her know I wouldn't be returning and the situation and she understood. I didn't want them to think I was a no-show, but low and behold, I was on my way three days later to campus but I wasn't able to be let back on the team which devastated me so at that point I didn't care what I did when I did it or how it happened.

My best friend who I met in college, Akemi, was my ace boon coon along with Krysten and Whitney. We were a force to be reckoned with; every and any party we were there, clubs we were there, but our names were tarnished because we didn't care, twerking everywhere on everybody and anybody. We had fun and I don't regret it but the fun came with consequences.

Somewhere down the line I had to figure out how to pay for my spring semester and since I was only seventeen in college, I really didn't know; but I later withdrew and moved to Georgia to live with my mom and attend Chattahoochee Technical College and continued to cheer and do what I love, run track. I promoted parties around the city, did street team work and was even a "So Icy Girl." I worked at a collection agency and everything seemed to be going good in 2008. Being in the night life you meet different people and in 2009, I met someone who balled to a new level.

Magic City Mondays, Velvet Room, Boom Service, you name it we went. He was older than me and in the drug game but he had wisdom that I appreciated at my age. Seeing someone ball on that level lit a fire under me and it started a chain reaction. Some girls who I knew through promoting knew about clubs up in South Carolina but I wasn't fully ready so I went to Kamal's 21, which lasted two days due to me working day shift, and I already had a day job, so after a week I agreed to go to South Carolina with them to Club Money and Club Presidential.

The money was everywhere but I was an amateur and I wasn't getting rained on, just sprinkles, so after two or three months of going I ended the whole dancing trial. In 2010 I ended up moving back to Florida and transferring schools to continue on the track to become a nurse, but that was just a back up plan-for medical school. After time passed I realized that I would need to choose a path. I had too many and it wasn't helping my goal.

After picking the Biology B.S. major it was settled that I would find alternate routes in American schools and funding. The year 2011 came with full force and I tried my hand at dancing again; this time it wasn't so bad since I had a taste of the scene before and Palm Beach was just a speck on its level.

I was going to school and dancing all the while doing part/full time work as a home health aide, so the money was great, really great. I could have saved up but it was coming so fast. I would hear about King of Diamonds [a Miami club] through media take out or in the dressing rooms, but the rumors of how much it cost kept me away. After less than a year of working in Palm Beach I got fed up and wanted my taste of King of Diamonds. I knew I could get hired, it was just a matter of going down to Miami and doing it, regardless of how much it was.

The same month Tip Drill fell off the pole I decided to go to try out. My audition was okay, no pole tricks, and I was hired. It was seven girls and only four of us made it.

I was excited and ready for a new chapter and I met a girl named Chicago who I ended up traveling with to different clubs in Tampa and Orlando. In K.O.D. and Hollywood Nights I was introduced to a lot of "Check Boys" and that also piqued my interest. After a year at K.O.D I applied to Medical School in the Caribbean, and spring 2013, I received an acceptance letter from a school in St. Maarten, but I deferred my enrollment to continue to make money and save up before I'd begin in the fall of 2013.

Summer 2013 is when it began: the Fraud, the Big Money, the trips, the everything. I paid for medical school with a scheme that was placed in my lap and it helped me even though I'm behind bars for it.

I started medical school fall of 2014 and in fall of

2016 I was in my clinical portion but a warrant stopped me from getting U.S. clinicals. It was arranged through the state judge to do a walk through. I was given a $15,000 dollar bond and with documents in hand I took a flight October 16th, 2016 to help further my medical career, not knowing that a federal indictment was waiting for me as well as a federal warrant. The airport officers didn't see it and when the sheriff's office came and ran a NCIC check, it would be them to find the federal warrant for Georgia. So I took a flight 10-16-2016 only to be incarcerated until 03-11-2020, but this charge will not hinder my dreams. If I have to start over in a U.S. Medical School, I will.

I have three years supervised release and a fire under me so strong lethal injection is the only thing that could stop my dreams. Time is that time, and this time gave me added goals, a careful eye, new friends, tested old friends and closer to family. Hopefully you read this and see that even in a bad situation you must keep a positive outlook on life because it's not over until the man above says it's over. And know laws I've become a skeptical person, you can't tell me anything if you can't show me proof. Black and White says a lot.

"Stand for something or fall for anything"

Denise Keaton
#14106-104

My book coming soon: 2019 Urban Fiction

08 18 2018

FINDING MYSELF

Jessica Nicholas

How I have the incredible privilege to share my life and experience. Well, I'm from the Island of Guam. I know you all wondering where Guam is, well Guam is at the Pacific Ocean side, close by Japan. My nationality is "Chamorro." I am forty-five years old. My life growing up was rough. I have five older sisters and three brothers. I'm the youngest girl in my family, total of nine. My mother and I didn't get along, she had a lot of jealousy of me because I'm Daddy's "little princess."

Everything started bad when I was in sixth grade. I had my first boyfriend; few of our friends, we started skipping school. It's so funny when we skipped school, we built "huts" for shelters in the boonie (jungle), we all chipped in to buy cigarettes, beer and food to cook, we even built a bar-b-q grill. So with all that fun, my mother came to school to get me and my brother for a doctor's appointment, well I was not in class. She went crazy with the staff. When I made it home, I got my first "beating."

She beat me with a thin stick and then used a belt when the stick broke. I was bleeding everywhere, my back and legs, so I call my dad to come home and help me. He saw me and had the *biggest* argument with my mom. Things calm down with my parents, I had to promise my dad I would not disrespect my mother, and stay in school.

Years went by and in eighth grade year I got into trouble again, I started hanging out with terrible young teens. Smoking cigarettes and drinking liquor, getting into fights with people, then break into old people's houses and steal money and things we wanted to take. My first fight I got jumped by three girls just to be in a group gang. I put two girls in the hospital with broken nose and arm, and bruises. The police arrested me and question me with my mother there, they release me to my mother, but she wanted them to take me in to Department of Youth Affairs (DYA) for "bad kids." But my father told her not to.

Ninth grade year was worse, I started my first drug, meth ("Ice"), always into fights, had a girl over the railing holding her by her long hair, beat her so bad that she ended up at the hospital. My parents came to school and picked me up. I was not allowed at any public school in the island.

So my dad told me I'm going to private school, "Bad Choice." I didn't last, they expelled me for arguing with the principal because I was smoking in the restroom. My last year of high school, 12th grade, I made it! I graduated the class of '89; I had to take night classes just to graduate on my year.

So after graduation, I got pregnant, got married to my high school sweetheart. He joined the Air Force (Military), station at Mass (Boston). We lived there for four years, and that was the worst experience of my life. My marriage was falling apart, I was a mess.

I had no stability in my mind and emotions. As a result, I was controlled by feelings which meant that my circumstances determined whether I was happy, sad, irritated or mad. It was a miserable way to live. It will end up coming out in some way and affect me mentally, emotionally. Divorce came along...

Years later I was drinking so much, always out clubbing and getting high (smoking meth). Did it for fifteen years, drugs was the only thing that kept me going, didn't care about anyone or anything, not even my kids. I will leave my kids with friends or my parents for weeks. I will steal from my mom and other family, just to support my habits and high...

I left Guam 2011 to better myself and start a new life with my four kids! I have a disabled daughter and I needed to work on getting her all the help she needed at Mainland. So we moved to Florida, just like Guam weather. We lived two years in Florida, then 2013 we moved to South Carolina, stayed with my niece for a while, then found a four-bedroom home, then life change to meeting a guy that abuse me, raped me, stoled from my kids and me. This relationship last for six months.

In 2016 I moved back to Florida (Tampa) with my family, then life changed again. I got married. We were living well, had good jobs and nice home and car. But me and my husband had done a crime. We robbed a gas station, got away with the money, within weeks pass he wanted more, so we went to do it again and my instinct told me not to, so we were leaving the gas station and not noticing that the supervisor was leaving the same time I was pulling out. We got pulled over and we were arrested, went to jail, got release on bail for nine months, then we both got sentenced May 2017. I'm in FCI Tallahassee, Florida serving fifty-seven months (four years and nine months).

It may seem strange, but the truth is you have a much more active relationship with yourself than you do with anyone else. Think about it, you can never get away from yourself; wherever you go, there you are! And if you don't like yourself, you're in for a miserable life.

Well, I spent many years being miserable because I didn't like myself. It started because of abuse that I experienced throughout my childhood, which caused a riot of shame to grow in my soul. I was ashamed of who I was…and it poisoned my soul. I lived as a broken Christian for a long time. But when I finally made the decision to do whatever I had to do, God could heal my soul.

I began a journey to wholeness that has radically changed my life. It wasn't easy and took longer than I thought it would take, but it was worth it to be able to live with peace and really enjoy my life. We all go through hard things and experience wounds in our soul and we all have a story to tell…The truth is, God wants you to enjoy your life, not just survive and live with the pain of your past. Once you have that foundation established, everything else falls into place.

Jessica Nicholas
#67470-018

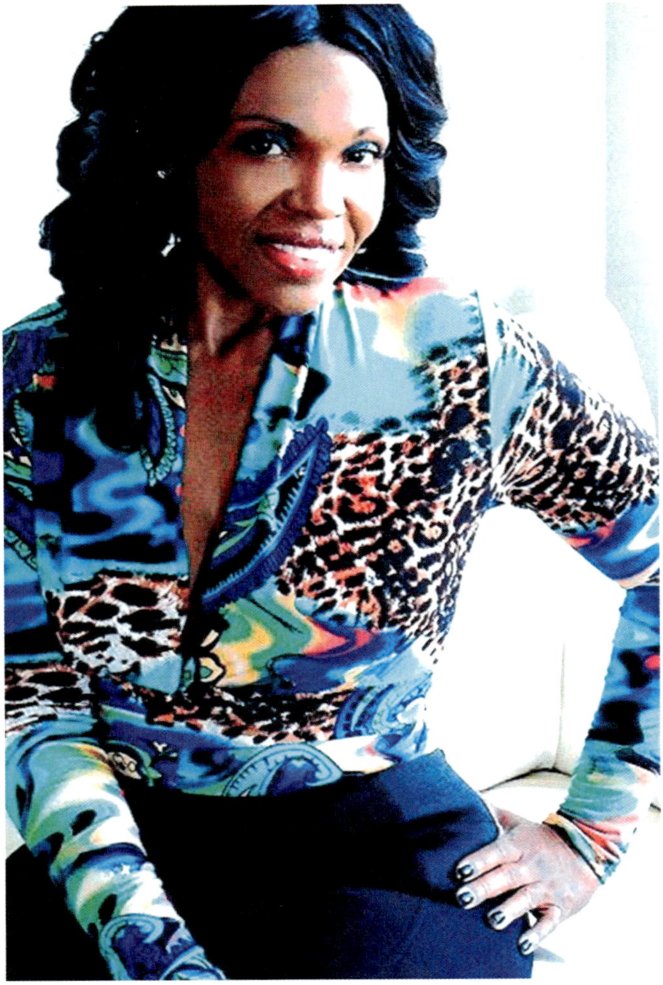

MY LIFE

Patrice Weber

First, giving honor to God who is the head of my life; without you I am nothing. You've been so good to me, better than I could ever be to myself. I can't begin to count all the times you've Blessed me, so if you never do anything else for me you have already done enough…

Second, to my Lord and Savior Jesus Christ, you have been my best friend. Many times in my life, when I was in trouble and I couldn't call on anyone else, I would call on Jesus and each time, Jesus showed up for me in ways I can't explain. Oh, how I love the name Jesus…

My favorite book is the Bible and I keep you close. You've been the lover of my soul and the answer to all my prayers. And to my Guardian Angels, how you protected me from the seen and unseen dangers in life. You slew all my giants, you crushed all my enemies, you kept all those hidden snakes away during times I was walking through the valley of the shadow of death and I feared no evil (Psalm 23), for you were right there with me, and for that I am forever grateful.

It's a privilege for me to be able to put "My Life" in a book, when I know that years ago I should've been dead... It's by God's grace I'm still standing, so I will not be ashamed of who I am, where I come from or what I have been through in life. This is my Testimony.

I was born and raised in a city that never sleeps, a city that loves to party and knows how to celebrate. I am a New Orleans, Louisiana native who speaks with a prideful New Orleans Cajun accent. My mother, Ruby, was a single parent who struggled to raised three children on her own. With the help of commodities (government foods), food stamps were how we ate, and welfare was all we had. Public housing is where we lived and all we could afford, and government assistance is how we survived.

I, along with my siblings, Henry and Georgia, grew up as a fatherless child, each one of us. No memories of a dad; no visits, no calls, no love and no support. How could we miss something we never had? All we had ever had and known was our mother.

Our mother was our father
&
Our father was our mother

We grew up in the projects of New Orleans, called the 9th ward area; some may call it the ghetto, while others may call it the hood. As kids, life was good for us, fun and adventurous, with so many friends in the neighborhood. My mother was a full-time mom, always available for us, and she never left our side. She did her best with the little she had. I was the oldest child of three, so my brother and sister looked up to me. At a very early age we were taught how to love one another, to honor and respect our mother and elders, that our days may be long on earth.

Going to church and to school was all I knew. My mother made sure of that, so she never had to wake me up for church or for school, I was born ready. I was excited about life and what life had to offer me. Even though at times, I was the hard-headed one, rebellious, wanting to do my own thang, but eventually I was chastised for my behavior. Throughout school I participated in just about everything. I was a team player, self-motivated and self-driven. I was determined.

Basketball, I played all positions
Track, I ran long distance (440, 880)
Talent Shows, I won different places (1st; 2nd; or 3rd)
Volleyball, I would spike on you
Swimming, I can—like a shark
Dancing Squad, I had the moves
Majorette was my favorite and I twirled two batons

I was a trophy girl; I brought home medals and certificates to my mom and filled up the living room with my awards. My mother was so proud of me, being that I was her oldest child. She knew that her daughter was going somewhere in life. My future was bright, I was full of potential and I had ambitions.

In 1991, my senior year, I only had three classes. Everything I wanted to do in school, I did! My mother supported me 100%. Even without help and support from my dad, she made sure I had everything that I needed. I had a lot of friends in the projects that I grew up with who were dropping out of school, having babies, and not making plans for the future; but I was the fortunate one out of the bunch who excelled at everything I put my mind to. I finished school and I had the opportunity to pursue my dreams.

Being an honor student, in honors classes, I had the opportunity to receive a scholarship to college for nursing; or maybe I could've gone to the WNBA for being the team player that I was. My mother suggested that I go into the military (U.S. Air Force) because she didn't want me to get caught up in the environment we were in. I said yes, took her advice, took the test and passed. But later on I changed my mind and settled for my passion, what I was gifted and talented in: cosmetology.

But I failed to chase my dreams. I made a major detour and went in a whole different direction. The "Boys in the Hood" who were in the dope game caught my attention. Seeing how they went from being broke to balling (getting rich). So I wanted what they had and were getting. I got involved with one dope boy after another. Before I knew it, I was in love with them and the game, and both relationships were too toxic for me. It made me forget my purpose in life and the reason why I had finished school. It was to better myself, so that I could have the opportunity to go further in life and to be able to get out of the hood, but the night life, nice cars, fast money and expensive clothes became my goals in life, day after day, chasing money, repeat again and again.

When I was in school, doing well and making good grades, my mother was my biggest fan, cheering me on and supporting me all the way. But then her cheering turned to praying and having the church pray for me. I started making poor choices in life and I was headed in all the wrong directions. The lifestyle I had chosen was not good for me and nothing good comes from that lifestyle.

> The hustling turned into the gambling
> The gambling turned into the clubbing
> The clubbing turned into the partying
> The partying turned into the drinking
> The drinking turned into the drugging

And my life started spiraling out of control. I went from Prom Queen to crack fiend! My life went from doing good things to doing bad; then it got ugly. My hobbies became my habits and I abused recreational drugs. I became famous for my reputation as a drug addict, but I thank God that I was loved by two uncles, Gregory and Theodore, who loved me in spite of this person I had become. They were told that I was hooked and abusing drugs, so they decided to come and get me, take me to Atlanta for me to change my lifestyle.

That was the best thing that they could've done for me, by moving me out of the environment that I had become. I had got caught up in everything I saw going on around me. The Bible had warned me that "Bad company will corrupt good character" and I went from winning to losing.

While living in Atlanta, I became pregnant with my first daughter, Chantice. I decided to move back home so my mother could show me how to be a mother. After I had Chantice in 1993, I picked up right where I had left off. I was back abusing drugs and the drugs were abusing me.

Eleven months later I gave birth to my second daughter, Shanice. My mother once told me these words: "Girl, you ain't give your first baby time to be the baby and you went and made another baby." So yes, I had my daughters back to back, '93 and '94.

New Orleans in the '90s became a city of drugs and violence and I became a prostitute to support my drug habits. My mother was forced to raise my daughters because I was not in my right frame of mind, unstable in all my ways. For many years drugs got the best of me. I lived to get high and I got high to live. One drug led to other drugs. I fell in love with the girl first, (cocaine, crack) then came the boy (heroin). I couldn't have one without the other.

At the beginning of my story, I stated that I will not be ashamed of who I am, where I come from or what I've been through in life. This is my Testimony. I've lost so many of my friends to drugs, AIDS and gun violence. So many of my friends didn't make it through the struggle, but I'm still here to tell you my story and to share my life with you. I'm not proud of my past but today I know that my past has a purpose.

The man of God I call my Pastor, who I look up to, who inspires me to be better and encourages me along the way through his weekly Ministry and his uplifting books, said these words, and I hold them close to my heart:

> "You are not defined by your past
> You are prepared by your past"

— Joel Osteen

I am grateful, because there were times in my life while

I was high on drugs I was caught up in the middle of shoot-outs and drug wars. I have also witnessed friends die from drug overdoses, right before my face, when that could've so easily been me. All I can say is that I'm blessed.

Just like a whirlpool, my life was going in circles; stealing and committing crimes, just to get high and support my drug habits, was my lifestyle. I was living recklessly and carelessly.

I couldn't understand why my mother would pray for me to go to jail. One day she helped me to understand her reason behind those prayers. She said to me, "Patrice, jail is the only place that can save you right now. I can come and visit you in jail but I can't come visit you in the grave."

Those words opened my eyes and hit me like a ton of bricks, and those words made me feel some type of way… a feeling that's hard to describe. So I started going to jail and that was the answer to my mother's daily prayers that God in his loving mercy would step in, rescue me, take me off the streets and change my life.

My first offense was in 1993, for possession of marijuana, and the following year I was convicted for forgery and sentenced to three years probation. Both charges were in New Orleans. I violated my probation in 1997 by going to Atlanta without permission and I got busted for drug charges. I only served four months in Atlanta and I was transferred back to New Orleans, to serve fifteen months for probation violation.

"When I could've been a teammate
I became an inmate"

— Patrice Weber

I continued with that vicious cycle, as if I didn't have any responsibilities, when I knew my family was relying on me. My mother never gave up on me, even though she was angry at this person I had become. She hated the way it made me look, how I was living, and she despised this monster I had become. The drugs kept me running because I was so ashamed of this person I had become.

At the age of twenty-eight, I gave birth to my third daughter, Caprice, while I was serving time in prison on violations, but three days later, after giving birth to my baby girl, I was released from prison. I didn't want to abandon my baby like I did with the other two by leaving my responsibility on my mother—again. So I made a conscious decision to seek help (long term treatment) for my substance abuse in a facility that would allow me to raise my baby with me, while I got help at the same time.

I was doing well, got my life back on track and I started having my oldest two daughters spend every weekend with me and my new baby. I was clean and living sober, going to school and working at the same time, while I was still living in the long-term treatment facility. The same year my daughter Caprice was born, my only brother, Henry, was sentenced to life in prison for murder. I felt like I just gave birth to a blessing and then a life was taken away, right before me.

Nobody ever told me, "Patrice, the road will be easy for you while traveling on this tedious journey." What I was told is to "Be strong and put your trust in the Lord."

So far, life has been a constant struggle for me and my family, with extreme highs and extreme lows, with one struggle after another.

August 29, 2005 came Hurricane Katrina; she was a

bad girl and right before my eyes I saw her destroy my city, my community, and I saw her take so many lives. I couldn't help them because I was trying to save myself. My mother and children went through a lot, trapped inside of the New Orleans, Louisiana Superdome for days; my sister and my nephew were stranded on top of a bridge and they had to be rescued. I was trapped in the 9th ward area right where the levees had broken, with my neighborhood friends, fighting for our lives. On that day the world felt our pain, and they saw us struggle to survive.

After that, my family and I faced the challenge of relocating to Houston, Texas. It was hard on us trying to mend back the broken pieces, but as a family we continued to weather life's storms. My mother is the true definition of a strong Black woman. She gives me hope and strength, with courage to keep fighting, to never give up, and to stay in the race no matter what may come our way.

My mother is a woman who came from nothing, but had faith. She never gave up on me, even when I was addicted and locked up. She raised me well, to the best of her ability, and she stepped up as my mother to raise my children as well. She believes without a shadow of a doubt that one day my brother will be free. She's lived through many storms in life. She is a fighter not with her hands, but with prayers, on her knees. With tears in my eyes I can say that I'm proud and I'm blessed to have her in my life as my mother. I just want to make my mother proud.

I love you, Ruby Mae Weber-Martin.

Throughout the years, we've been traveling back and forth from Houston to New Orleans to visit our loved ones and to go see my brother in Angola Penitentiary. While traveling west on 610 from New Orleans back to

Houston, there's a sign that warns us Louisiana people "Don't Mess with Texas"…and I've found that statement to be true. Since living in Texas, I've been convicted on ten felony charges, more than I've ever been convicted of in my own city, New Orleans.

But in 2009 I was introduced to a brand new way of getting money in Texas, and this time it wasn't in the streets. This profession was for a Professional Licensed Nurse, something I once wanted to be, when I finished high school. I fell in love with my new-found hustle/job in healthcare that brought in cash by recruiting patients with Medicare. This hustle/job was good and safe, so I thought, making anything from $1,500-$5,000 a week or more, tax free. It was easy for me being the hustler and the go-getter that I was, but I didn't just recruit patients, I also recruited someone that I love, my sister, and a few others who were close to me, because it was easy, fast and enough for all of us to make money, so they joined the team.

Until 2014, when the Feds started their investigation into me. I knew God was always watching over me, but so were the Feds…so I had to co-operate with them—this was the federal government. Anytime you mention those alphabet boys, such as FBI, DEA, ATF, or the IRS, that meant business and something serious, nothing to play with. Nothing like the State, which I was so familiar with; this was much bigger than the norm. The Feds stated that the company I was employed by cheated the government out of four million dollars and I was a part of that operation.

So on January 26, 2015, I can remember it like yesterday, I pleaded guilty to one count of conspiracy to commit healthcare fraud. I need to say I was scared for my life; this wasn't anything like the State, this was the big boys (the Feds) whose hands my life was in. I was on pretrial release for two years, until my sentencing date. I was charged with 1.5 million of those dollars, out of that four million dollars, so I guess you can say that I'm a "millionaire"; but with my plea agreement it was dropped down to $928,259.61 (criminal monetary penalties) that I owe back to the government. And they mean business, you *will* pay that money back to the government.

"What's understood don't need to be explained"

I'm here today in FCI, Tallahassee, serving thirty-six months in federal prison. Once again, my hands go up to the man up above, who is in heaven, from which all my blessings flow. I won't complain about thirty-six months, when I could've so easily gotten anything from a seven- to a ten-year bid just from my prior criminal history, but for Jesus.

Since serving time in federal prison, I've grown in many ways and I've turned my life around in positive ways. Upon being rehabilitated from drug addictions and successfully completing twenty-one life-changing programs, my education transcript looks better than my criminal rap sheet. Now I'm better prepared with the knowledge and tools that I need to win and succeed in life. What was meant for my bad is working for my good.

Today, I am a Theologian student at International Christian College and Seminar (ICCS). I'm just a few credits away from receiving my associate's degree in Ministry, while serving time in prison. There's nothing in life you can't do once you put your heart, mind and soul into it; the impossible becomes possible.

My life has been an open book since I was born, so this is just an introduction to what's next. I am currently working on publishing several other books besides this one. I have no doubt that my new and healthy lifestyle will be greatly beneficial upon my release as I reconnect with my family and optimistically deal with the tough roads that lie ahead.

Today, I know who I am and where I'm going: I am a woman with purpose and there's a reason why I'm living. It ain't over until God says it's over. I am a phenomenal woman, who is capable of turning her struggles into stairs, and build on until I reach my highest peak.

Thanks for allowing me to share a percentage of "My Life" with you.

Stay Tuned…

Patrice Weber
#80952-379

ABOUT PATRICE WEBER

Patrice Weber is a New Orleans, Louisiana native who looks more like a "Housewife of Atlanta" than an inmate. She has served a combined term in both state and federal prison. While serving a thirty-six-month sentence at the Tallahassee, FL federal prison she began turning her life around in positive ways. She successfully completed twenty-one life-changing programs that will be greatly beneficial upon her release, and this has helped her grow spiritually, academically and professionally.

During the time she was incarcerated, Patrice has earned her associate degree in Ministry at the International Christian College and Seminary (ICCS) as a stellar student, excelling in all required courses. Patrice aspires to continue her studies in Ministry until she receives her Doctorate degree and becomes Dr. Patrice Weber.

She has found her passion and new love in writing and is currently working on publishing several books. Patrice came to believe that if she wanted to make a difference (M.A.D.), in the lives of people, she had to be the difference.

Made in the USA
Columbia, SC
23 July 2022